Become a Better Leader,
10 Minutes at
a Time

Jeff Harmon

New Jersey and enjoy trying new restaurants, swimming, family games, and serving the Lord together.

Jeff is available as a private leadership coach, keynote speaker, workshop leader and servant leadership resource. Contact him at +1-201-294-4417 or *Jeff@BrillianceWithinCoaching.com* for further details.

ISBN-13: 978-0-9910161-0-5

What People Are Saying...

" Simple, practical strategies in bite-sized, 10-minute segments. Harmon's latest work is a must-read for the busy manager or leader on the go. Helpful business illustrations, practical applications, dynamic tools, and thought-provoking questions help us become better leaders, 10 minutes at a time."

Dr. Jeff Daniels
Chief information security officer
Associate professor

" Don't be deceived by the thinness of this book. It is THICK with real world examples and common sense approaches to leading organizations with a servant leadership approach. I'm envisioning using this with several organizations that I work with."

Jeff Miller
Innovative Leadership Solutions
Greenleaf Center for Servant Leadership Academy faculty
member

" Jeff clearly demonstrates that effective leadership requires more than skills and intention; it requires the proper mindset as well. The good news is that most leaders already possess and use this mindset in other parts of their lives and they can bring it to their professional work with the 10-Minute

Leadership approach. *Become a Better Leader, 10 Minutes at a Time* is full of practical wisdom. Give yourself the gift of reading it. I did."

Rev. James H. Latimer, ACC
Founder of StrongStartCoaching
Church pastor and coach to pastors and business professionals

" Jeff provides insight and motivation through tiny chapters that speak volumes. Learning how Mike McCarthy responded to terrible circumstances with kindness and grace helps me see potential in myself to react better when people make mistakes or things don't go my way. Invest in yourself by reading this short book."

Mark Gavagan
Entrepreneur and public speaking expert

Table of Contents

Introduction.. 2

Section One: Mindset..**5**

Building a Leadership Foundation............................ 6

Leadership Starts With Love 9

Why Parents are Naturally Good Leaders 12

Leading on Purpose.. 16

Live in the Vision.. 20

Section Two: Practical Leadership
Strategies **25**

Notice, Wonder, Question, Play – An Unlikely
Leadership Formula.. 26

Notice – Just Pay Attention................................... 27

Wonder and Question – Curiosity is a
Childhood Skill That's Worth Re-Learning......... 29

Play – Play Turns Work to Fun 31

Be Tough on the Problem, Gentle on the Person ... 35

6.5 Ways to Energize People..................................... 39

WHASSUP – Take Your Leadership on a Walk 43

Strategic Thinking Time is a Must 48

Can You Be a Leader 10 Minutes at a Time? 52

Conclusion: The Final Word...........................**56**

About Jeff Harmon..**58**

Introduction

The reality for most leaders in the 21st century is we have tasks and objectives of our own to tackle, all while leading others to accomplish the vision of the business or organization. Very few of us can actually spend all our time leading, and our own leadership development is often relegated to on the job training.

For most of my clients, our coaching sessions are the only times they spend in strategic thinking and leadership development. I'm supporting them to build an environment where this isn't the case, and it's a process to evolve both the leader and the organization to get there. In the meantime, becoming a better leader that empowers people, inspires innovation and creativity, and generates commitment and powerful results happens in small intervals – sometimes as little as 10 minutes at a time.

The foundation of my personal leadership approach, as described here and in my first book, The Anatomy of a Principled Leader, is a principled, character driven one called servant leadership. This approach has been called "soft" and not results focused, however servant leadership is actually all about results. The difference is in seeing yourself as being there for your people and not them being there for you in the achievement of those results.

This book is a selection of blog posts from the last three years that speak to the mindset and practices of a principled, serving leader. As you spend 10 minutes at a time with me, reading one or more sections of this book, I hope this puts you on a path to achieve the results that are most important to you, not only through your own efforts, but also by the efforts of those you are leading.

Section One:
Mindset

Building a Leadership Foundation

Fourteen years ago, I was almost fired from my job. At that early stage of my career, I was suffering from "young person's disease," whose symptoms include over-confidence (bordering on cocky), defensiveness and an unwillingness to admit mistakes. "Relax, I got this covered," was my favorite saying.

Luckily, I've matured and grown since then, and I've discovered the importance of humility. Some of the greatest successes in my career have been born out of an apology even when I felt that I was right. Not only have I built friendships out of those experiences, but also tremendous allies in delivering high-quality results. Without humility, those project successes would have been much more difficult to achieve.

As a leader, when my focus shifted from the team being in service to me to me being of service to my team, I saw that my role now included administrator, coordinator, director, coach, facilitator and expeditor. I like the analogy of the leader being like the bumpers in a bowling lane; we protect the team and the project, and keep the ball rolling down the lane.

Leadership success starts with humility and I can see how the track record of my success followed the evolution of my humility. The more humble I became, the more success I realized. AMAZING! This humility in leadership led to my desire to invest in and develop others and put people first.

Thank you for demonstrating the humility to pick up this book and be open to new ideas that will strengthen your leadership.

⏱ 10-Minute Leadership Questions:

- *What role will you add to your leadership job description to be of service to your team?*

- *Who will you talk with to learn about what others feel about your level of humility?*

Journal

_____

_____

_____

_____

_____

_____

_____

_____

_____

_____

_____

_____

_____

_____

_____

_____

Leadership Starts With Love

Love is undoubtedly a powerful leadership tool. It is the force behind humility, listening, our commitment to developing others, and many other character-based behaviors that have an impact on the health of a team or organization.

How, though, can you convince someone to have a feeling or emotion for someone else? Why is it so difficult to bring love to work?

That question has remained unanswered for me until I read *The Servant: A Simple Story about the True Essence of Leadership* by James Hunter and came upon this simple phrase that gave me amazing insight: "Love is a verb, not a noun."

This phrase blew me away with its elegant simplicity. Read it again and think about it for a minute.

As a noun, love is a feeling. A feeling deep in your being that is palpable. It's often hard to describe it exactly, but you know when it's there. Love for spouse, friends, pets, children, your favorite football team. We generally associate love with positive feelings.

As a noun, the opportunity and possibility to bring love to leadership is very limited. How many things or people in your professional life do you have feelings of love towards? When I think of my own work, I can honestly say that I don't feel love towards most people or things. I care about people, but I would not define that feeling as love.

The truth is that there are some people I lead who I don't really like very much and I disapprove of their behavior. I definitely don't feel love towards them. If I were to wait for the feeling of love to motivate my investment in them, my humility towards them or listening would never come.

As a verb though, love is something different. In Greek, there is the verb *agapao* to describe an unconditional love that is rooted in behavior towards others without regard to what they are due or deserve. You may not be able to control how you feel about other people, but you certainly control how you behave toward them. Feelings may come and go based on any number of factors, but I can still behave lovingly. I can listen, be humble and put that distasteful person's development as a priority, even though he or she chooses to behave poorly.

This "a-ha" moment has given me insight into love and leadership, but it certainly doesn't make it easier. As Hunter says in the book, it takes a tremendous amount of will to behave lovingly. Leadership is work and this is one area where I think I'll be working for the rest of my life.

 10-Minute Leadership Questions:

- *Who do you not particularly care for who would benefit from a little love?*

- *What would love look like in that situation?*

Journal

Why Parents are Naturally
Good Leaders

When a child is born, what is a parent's first instinct? (Right after they weep openly or freak out that they have a little human to take care of.) My wife and I immediately had the natural instinct to love, care, serve and support the needs of this life that had been entrusted into our care.

We didn't make a choice in this; the inclination to serve as a parent came naturally. Even when our children are challenged or challenging in some way, we love them and work to create an environment where they can thrive.

What does any of this have to do with leading an organization? Everything! It's time to question why we leave who we are as Mom or Dad at home and turn into our "work self" when we walk through the door of our jobs.

We also leave behind that loving, caring, serving nature that is so instinctual to us as parents. We temper the natural instinct to love to the point where it is watered down and unusable.

Yet our teams, employees, peers and bosses are people, just like our kids. They aren't a steel pipe that pumps out work. They thrive when they're nurtured and loved, just like our kids.

It's NOT just love for love's sake. You're not detached from the results. Just as you know that the love you invest in your kids will increase the chance for a successful and fulfilling life, you can expect that the love you invest as a leader will lead to a productive, fulfilling and successful business experience.

The following three elements of leadership mindset will prepare you to tap into your loving, serving nature and transform how you show up at work:

1. **Unlimited liability**

   Start to assume unlimited liability for those you lead. Love them unconditionally, just like your kids. Organizations today are guided to mitigate risk and assume limited to no liability. Turn that norm on its head and provide unconditional support and care for those you lead. Then watch their trust, respect and creativity soar. (Also see *Section Two, Tough on the Problem, Gentle on the Person.*)

2. **Listening**

   Parents of teenagers know that your kids aren't always in the mood to talk. So when they are, you'd better be ready to listen or you might miss a valuable opportunity. Your natural instinct to serve responds to any problem by first listening. True listening builds strength in other people and you'll receive all the insights you need to set the right course.

3. Teaching

Remember when you taught your son or daughter to ride a bike? You didn't sit them down at the kitchen table, explain the ins and outs of riding a bike and then send them on their way. You took them outside, placed them on the bike and then ran next to them until they could do it on their own. Next time you give an assignment, walk next to the person for a while and support him or her to succeed.

This week, bring the Mom or Dad in you to work, so you can serve and love in your leadership.

 10-Minute Leadership Questions:

- *What assignment will you give this week where you can walk alongside for a while?*

- *What assumptions about your team do you need to get rid of to take unlimited liability for them?*

Journal

Leading on Purpose

In a recent conversation about his business, someone said to me that, "my purpose is to sell my business for a profit in 10 years." Nothing wrong with that, yet through our conversation his REAL purpose was revealed. What he really loves, he said, is tinkering with other people's stuff and helping them get the most out of their assets. Now that's a purpose to hang your hat on.

Dan Pink said in his book *Drive* that "the most deeply motivated people—not to mention those who are most productive and satisfied—hitch their desires to a cause larger than themselves." Money just doesn't have the same power to motivate as purpose does and when you or your business stands for something of greater significance in the world than just profit, you'll start to achieve more than you might have anticipated.

Use these three strategies to intentionally make purpose part of doing business every day:

1. Communicate your purpose with stories

Every organization has a story to tell and the most powerful stories usually involve people who begin with a dream, encounter challenges and crises and learn from them. Stories paint the picture of why you do what you do (i.e., your purpose) and become a part of the glue that unifies an organization, helping you and your followers remain true to their purpose and values as well as celebrate the evolution of the organization.

As a leader, the most important story you tell is probably your own. In *The Leader's Voice* by Ron Crossland and Boyd Clarke, leaders are encouraged to "make sure the words are yours. Push them from the very bottom of your soul. The performance will take care of itself." Storytelling is a great way to communicate your business's or organization's purpose.

2. **Shift the leadership focus from profit to purpose**

A client recently shared with me that her business had reached a plateau. Although they have been successful, she realized that she's not even sure if her employees and volunteers really get what the business is all about. They do what she asks, but it seems like work has turned into something they check off their to-do list at the end of the day.

My client is very passionate about her organization's purpose to serve some of the neediest people in our area. What if she could reinvigorate her team with that passion and get them as devoted to the purpose as she is?

When your team can say, "I know why we do what we do and I believe in it," a shift takes place where *they no longer work for you or the bottom line, they work for the purpose.* This makes them partners in your shared work and gives everyone a compass to follow.

3. Be flexible with your purpose

CEO of IBM Ginni Rometty recently commented that her predecessor "taught us, above all, that we must never stop reinventing IBM." Even the biggest of the big like IBM realize that businesses must evolve with the times. Make it part of the annual review of your business to examine its purpose and ensure that you, your employees and your strategy are aligned. Is the purpose you had defined still right for today? Is it still why you do what you do? If not, get out the sandpaper and smooth off the rough edges.

Having a purpose gives EVERYONE in your organization a place to hang their hat. It is an awesome thing when everyone in your organization can say, "I understand what we're doing," "I believe in what we're doing" and "I know why we are doing it."

When everyone can make these declarations (and mean them), that means you have created a line of sight between your business' purpose and every person, job and role. Without this clear line of sight, you are left to deal with a disengaged and directionless workforce.

 10-Minute Leadership Questions:

- *Why do you do what you do every day?*

- *What's the greater purpose for your work and your life?*

Journal

Live in the Vision

Football seems to be a treasure trove of examples of principled leadership in action, when we examine the interaction between players and coaches on the field, in practice and in the locker room. Here is an example from a professional football coach that cements the right leadership mindset:

When Chuck Pagano was in his first year as head coach of the Colts, the team was also led at quarterback by a rookie. Three games into that 2012 season, Coach Pagano was diagnosed with leukemia and immediately took a leave of absence to begin treatment.

Pagano's fighting spirit inspired the team early in the season to an impressive victory over the highly favored Green Bay Packers. One Sunday in November 2012, the Colts took the field against the Miami Dolphins and came away with another hard fought victory after being down in the final minutes.

Pagano, who was in between treatment cycles, attended the game and addressed the team before and after the game. His post-game speech was caught by the cameras, and you can watch the speech here:

http://www.youtube.com/watch?v=3I9UsfDZLyQ

It could be easy to get caught up in the emotion of the moment (and believe me I did) but there is also a powerful example of principled leadership in action.

The two characteristics of a principled leadership mindset that Pagano displayed are represented by the eyes and feet. Principled leaders have the ability to see out ahead, beyond the circumstances of the moment. They not only see the direction, mission and end goal, they are also able to ground their feet and the team's feet in that vision.

They do not allow themselves to get held back by their circumstances or what others say those circumstance should mean to the team. For the Colts football team, this means not getting hung up by what the prognosticators and media said "should" happen to a team that only won two games the year before and has a new coach and rookie quarterback. Those are just circumstances and they are refusing to be defined by those, but are rather living in the vision of a championship.

For Pagano, this means not getting dragged into the stereotype of what the circumstances might dictate for a cancer patient living through treatment. Instead, he's living in the vision of dancing with his daughters at their weddings and lifting a championship trophy with his team. That vision is what is defining him, not the circumstances he's living through.

🕐 10-Minute Leadership Questions:

- *What circumstances are presently defining your mood, attitude and behavior in your leadership setting?*

- *What is the bigger vision you have for your work?*

- *What steps will you take to ground your feet and point your eyes to that vision every day?*

Journal

_____

_____

_____

_____

_____

_____

_____

_____

_____

_____

_____

_____

_____

_____

Section Two:
Practical Leadership
Strategies

Notice, Wonder, Question, Play – An Unlikely Leadership Formula

Inspiration can come from anywhere.

During a short family vacation to Boston and southern Maine, a jolt of inspiration came from the Boston's Children's Museum. (First, a plug for the museum. It was an awesome place for kids and adults alike. I highly recommend it, especially for those with children. Now, on to the inspiration.)

As I was strolling along, watching my daughter become drawn in by all the hands-on exhibits I was drawn to the John Hancock Science Playground. What drew me was the motto of the area, "Notice, wonder, question, play." So simple, but profound in the possibilities for anyone who would apply those four words to whatever station in life you find yourself.

For kids, this motto makes total sense, especially in a learning environment. Kids absorb the most and are at their most creative when they are free to let their natural curiosity roam, to ask lots of questions, and to play in that space without fear of making mistakes or getting it wrong. The application for those in a position of leadership may not be so obvious, yet that is exactly where my mind went.

The role of a leader, especially those who choose to serve through leadership, is to empower those being served – to leave them wiser, freer, and more autonomous through every encounter. What better way to accomplish this than to honor each of the four parts of the motto, "Notice, wonder, question, play?"

Let's look at each of the four parts of this motto and its practical application to your leadership.

Notice – Just Pay Attention

Throughout the Boston Children's Museum are exhibits that challenge the children (and adults) to first and foremost just notice: the big hula-hoop that produced even bigger bubbles, the mini roller coaster where golf balls were propelled up, down and around, and the lever system attached to a seat that allowed my 40-pound daughter to lift her own weight.

The intention was not for the kids to "figure it out" but to simply notice what was happening. In the noticing are the seeds to learning, new discoveries, and a depth of understanding that couldn't be achieved through teaching alone. At the museum, the questions of how or why the exhibits worked were abandoned in favor of, "What's happening here?", "What do you see?", and "How does it feel?"

Woody Allen once said that 80% of success is just showing up. I'd like to propose that 80% of success is just paying attention. How many times have you been in a situation where if you had just noticed what was happening around you, you could have either averted disaster or been a hero?

Here's an example:

The head of a publishing company had a practice of writing personal notes to his people – he wanted them to see that he was following along with what has happening outside of the executive offices. When one of his employees became the first person to win the Iowa lottery (her winnings were $5,000), he wrote, "Hope you won't take your money and leave because we need you around here." Several years later at his retirement ceremony that same employee greeted him in the receiving line with tears in her eyes. She told him, "I'll never forget that note. It meant so much to me." What power in just paying attention.

So much of leadership is about paying attention. It's really as simple as letting go of the why and how for a few minutes, and focusing on what's actually happening. So what are the traps that keep us from noticing what's going on around us?

1. **Laziness**

   We can fall into a lull of thinking, "I'm doing enough." This complacency can happen in a household, a church, or a Fortune 500 company. We stop asking questions like "What am I seeing here?" or "How am I feeling?" or "How are other people feeling?" And then because we're not looking for them, we stop noticing the clues (and often the answers) that are right in front of us.

2. Pressure of the moment

Our culture puts immense pressure on figuring things out and having the answer immediately. Little time is afforded to just sit with something and notice what it is and how it's working. People don't notice because they are busy trying to solve problems first. Really we need to re-order that sequence: first notice what's going on, then seek input, listen to the input, and then apply what we've learned to create a solution to the problem.

So as you venture into your leadership territory today, whether as a mom, pastor or CEO, notice what's happening. Sit with the questions for a while. Not only will you gain new and interesting insights, but your team, family or congregation will appreciate the fact that you're paying attention.

Wonder and Question – Curiosity is a Childhood Skill That's Worth Re-Learning

People have a natural desire to know more. You can hear it in the constant questioning of young children. Early learning begins with wonder, which turns to curiosity, inquiry and then knowledge, which yields an ever-deeper wonder. The people who designed the Boston Children's Museum definitely tapped into this. As we wandered through the exhibits, my daughter's innocent question, "But why, Daddy?" floated up to us over and over again with lightness and ease.

For the most part, my wife and I reward this curiosity. For many children, however, this natural curiosity often gets shut down, as adults begin to feel annoyed by the constant barrage of questions and challenges. Over time, children start looking for the "right" answer, instead of expressing their natural state of inquisitive wonder and openness to exploring all possible answers.

Exploration and possibility is also a powerful place for a leader. And it's not always easy to stay there. In leadership situations, my tendency was to spiral into attack mode when a question, problem or issue was presented. I even made a "STAY CURIOUS" sign to hang above my desk to stop me from immediately resorting to problem solving mode.

Feelings like survival, danger, judgment and fear would start to pop up. My wife says it's because I'm a male. She might be right, but I tend to think all humans are rewired at some point in life to find THE answer and find it quick.

Staying curious requires being disconnected from the outcome and open to the possibilities of what could be. It is the task of the leader to continually invite the follower/employee into curiosity by creating the environment and listening for innovation and uniqueness in the leader/follower conversation.

Here are three ways to re-ignite childhood curiosity in the workplace:

1. **Refocus**

   When you feel the urge to immediately go to problem solving mode, put your hand over your heart and take a deep breath. This will refocus you and remind you that your role as leader is to empower people and make them more autonomous. What's it going to cost you to remain open and curious, maybe five or ten extra minutes? In the grand scheme of things, that's a small price to pay for the benefits you'll both receive.

2. **Opt to listen**

   Avoid the temptation to evaluate or analyze what the person is saying. Keep listening. Don't interrupt, but rather offer the person words of encouragement. Phrases like "I see," "That's interesting," "Then what?" or "Tell me more" all invite the person to keep speaking and keeps you in curiosity mode.

3. **Ask questions**

   There are many types of questions and curiosity-based questions have one intention – to empower the person on his or her journey towards the goal that led the person to approach you. In the words of Robert Greenleaf, you want to leave them "wiser, freer and more autonomous."

Even if you don't start out feeling very curious, the good news is that when we act as if we are curious, soon we will be curious. If you find it uncomfortable to be curious (and you probably will), remember you have been this way since you were in elementary school, you just need to remember how to do it!

It's well worth the effort. Organizations that encourage curiosity accelerate learning and creativity and ultimately create a better business result.

Play – Play Turns Work to Fun

The power of play has been central to child development for centuries, but somehow, like the other childhood skills I shared in this series, play has fallen to the wayside in our adult world. That's a real shame, given that nearly 75% of workers today are disengaged. Play might just be one of the most powerful leadership tools that could pull us out of this rut.

Even in a child's world, it's amazing the difference it can make when you shift from work to play. In a famous Russian study from the 1950's, children were told to stand still as long as they could. They lasted two minutes. Then a second group of children were told to pretend (play) that they were soldiers on guard who had to stand still at their posts. They lasted eleven minutes.

In 2011, during the clean-up efforts after Hurricane Irene, I tapped into the power of play to make a potentially horrible day of back-breaking work into fun. The town assigned me a group of high school seniors to gut a flood-ravaged house down to the foundation and studs. This primarily meant tearing out wall boards or drywall.

I huddled the kids together and said since this was already a depressing situation with difficult work ahead, why not make a game out of the cleanup?

First we had the challenge of seeing who could break off the biggest piece of drywall. We kept a little "wall of fame" to showcase the largest pieces. Next we decided to see what US state the pieces of drywall most resembled (we found Utah, Oklahoma and Arkansas). Our backs were sore by the end of the day, but we laughed a lot and the entire job was done.

In a recent TED Talk by Dan Pink, he pointed to the power of play at work at an Australian software company named Atlassian. Once a quarter, the management at Atlassian tells the workers to take the next 24 hours to do whatever they want, with whoever they want. The only criterion is they have to show everyone what they did.

At the end of the 24 hours, they have a big "show and tell" event with beer and cake, where everyone gets to show off what they did.

The results are amazing. In this one day, new ideas for products and changes are created and problems that previously defied fixing are fixed. This one day of play produces things that would have otherwise not emerged.

The idea of play has classically only found its way into our workplaces as a form of staff development or to create more camaraderie during occasional company picnics, bowling outings, team lunches or happy hours. Those are important and have definite value in the work setting AND what I'm suggesting here is the integration of play into HOW you work.

Some of the inherent qualities of play are lightness, laughter, fun and autonomy. All of these are sources of motivation and of a healthier, more effective workplace.

🕐 10-Minute Leadership Questions:

- *What did you notice about your team over the last two days?*

- *What situation or person are you wildly curious about and what will you do about it?*

- *Where can you start to integrate play into HOW you and your team do work?*

Journal

_____

_____

_____

_____

_____

_____

_____

_____

_____

_____

_____

_____

_____

_____

_____

Be Tough on the Problem, Gentle on the Person

By now, even the casual football fan is aware of the situation that took place in Seattle in September 2012 where a referee awarded a touchdown to the Seattle Seahawks instead of an interception to the Green Bay Packers, a decision that gave Seattle the win. In the high stakes world of professional football, this botched judgment call led to a whirlwind of debate and fervor over the competency of the game officials.

As some might say is justified, the fans and players for the Packers rained down on the league and the refs with all sorts of unpleasantness and anger.

At his post-game press conference, Mike McCarthy, the head coach of the Packers, was immediately questioned about the scenario and the call by the officials that cost his team a victory in a sport where every victory is crucial to overall success in the season.

McCarthy showed great restraint and refused to evaluate the official's ruling or question his judgment. He simply wouldn't talk about it, even though you could see on his face that he vehemently disagreed with the call and was bitterly disappointed.

The next day McCarthy's character showed again after the league upheld the official's call. McCarthy still refused to throw the official under the bus.

The final show of character and the true example of principled leadership in action was a phone call McCarthy made to the official several days later. The official had been besieged at his home with anger-filled and threatening voicemails. The message McCarthy left was different. He told the official that he had heard he was having a rough time and that even though he didn't agree with the call, he wanted him to know that he thought he had handled the entire situation with dignity.

This is a person that McCarthy may never have to deal with or cross paths with again.

What were the two key elements of servant leadership in action displayed by Coach McCarthy?

1. **Silence is golden**

   In the face of disappointment, failure or situations falling short of expectations, where someone else is at fault, principled leaders don't pretend the problem didn't occur or hide their disappointment, but they also don't go into attack mode. Rather, they choose to remain silent about the person at fault.

2. **Endless compassion**

   Principled leaders in action extend themselves to the individual(s) involved and seek to build them up, acknowledge them, brush them off, and encourage them to move forward.

A principled leader is tough on the problem and gentle on the person.

⏰ 10-Minute Leadership Questions:

- *What challenge or issues are you facing right now that could use some golden silence?*

- *Who needs to be brushed off and encouraged after a recent mess-up?*

Journal

6.5 Ways to Energize People

Unless you work for a utility or oil company, energy in business is only about one thing: PEOPLE. Energy comes from mastery, empowerment, creativity, teamwork, love, empathy and acknowledgement. Money may also show up on this list somewhere, but it certainly isn't at the top of my list. Money by itself is like a mid-afternoon cup of coffee or Snickers bar. It gives you that immediate boost you might need, but it wears off in short order.

Instead, try one of these 6½ ways to energize your people:

1. **Show them the way**

   Cast a compelling vision of where you are going. People may desire to be empowered to chart their own course, but they still look to the leader to paint a beautiful picture of where they are going.

2. **Love them**

   No, not rainbows and puppy dog love. The love a leader has for his or her people is made of patience, kindness, generosity, courtesy, humility, unselfishness, good temper and sincerity. You can be all those things without sacrificing anything in the way of firmness and conviction.

3. Tell them your story

Tell your people what you believe in and why what you are doing matters. Tell them about your struggles and your dreams. In doing so you become human. Your people will be able to connect with you in unexpected ways. Your story will communicate your purpose and values in a way that a plaque with a mission statement printed never could.

4. Invest in them

People are inherently motivated by the opportunity to become masterful in something. By investing in developing your people and freeing them to develop themselves you energize them and they in turn energize your business.

5. Walk with them

In *The One Minute Manager*, Ken Blanchard writes: "People with humility don't think less of themselves; they just think of themselves less." Get out of your office and walk with your people. Walking with them doesn't only mean listening to what they have to say, but also celebrating, grieving and learning with them.

6. Remind them

Max DePree, former chairman of Herman Miller and author of *Leadership Is an Art*, compared the strategic role of a leader to that of a 3rd grade teacher who keeps repeating the basics: "When it comes to vision, values and direction, you have to say it over and over

and over again until people get it right, right, right."
A leader is consistently reminding his people of what
they're doing, why they're doing it and why it's
important.

6½.Remind them again and then let them get to the business of doing it

Any investment you make in energizing your people
will bring many returns. It actually becomes self-
generating after a while. Tapping into the energy
source of your people can be hard work AND it will
sustain you for the long haul.

10-Minute Leadership Questions:

- *What gives your people energy?*
  (Here's a tip: If you're not sure, ask them!)

- *What gives you energy?*

Journal

WHASSUP – Take Your Leadership on a Walk

A client of mine and his team had completed a series of assessments that we were using to understand where he was as a leader, from his own perspective and his team's.

He set out on this journey committed to his own growth as a leader and emphatic that his growth would benefit his team and the organization.

The themes that emerged from this process will be familiar to leaders of entrepreneurial ventures, things like vision, direction, delegation and communication.

In a recent coaching session to discuss how he would implement this feedback, my client's brilliance and personality emerged as he proceeded to lay out his action plan. Every time he said the name of the strategy, he said it with all the gusto of the Budweiser commercial from years ago: "WHASSUP!"

Watch the commercial here:

http://www.youtube.com/watch?v=UDTZCgsZGeA

Here's the WHASSUP strategy:

Walk – Get out of your office and walk around. Walk
the floor where your team members are,
stopping at the coffee station or wherever
employees hang out. By breaking down both
the visible and invisible barriers that separate
leader from follower, you eliminate any feeling
of us versus them and create a team
atmosphere.

Hear – Listen to what folks are talking about, what
their concerns are, and their unique perspective
on work, life and the world. Being silent and
simply listening shows respect for others and
encourages them to keep talking.

Ask – Ask open-ended question to go deeper into the
things you heard. Remain curious and
genuinely interested in their viewpoints. You'll
be surprised by what you learn and the
insights you'll gain. Be careful not to try to fix
situations or problems that might be
mentioned. Staying interested and curious by
asking questions will create trust and establish
a real "open door" environment.

See – Take notice of how people work, how they
work together, and the flow of work. You'll
start to see people's strengths and notice
opportunities to put people in the right spots to
improve how things get done.

Speak– Share what's on your mind what you've heard, seen and learned. Speak about where you see the group heading and the vision of what everyone is accomplishing together. This keeps an open dialogue going and everyone's eye on the mission and vision of the team.

Update –Get and give updates about ongoing work, or answers to questions from other meetings or conversations. This further enhances the trust among the team and ensures people feel safe and that there aren't any hidden agendas. This opens things up for creativity, deeper commitment, and innovation.

Play – Have fun, whether with work-related tasks or generally creating a playful, yet respectful, atmosphere. This further advances a culture of innovation and creates an environment where people want to be.

Here's what my client had to say about the impact:

> "The physical act of walking over allows me to break away from the current stream of client fires and business priorities to refocus my attention on the team or the individual I speak with. I feel like that short interaction is also a reinforcement of my accessibility to all, that people can have access to me by doing the same. Lastly, I believe that enthusiasm and positivity are contagious so each interaction gives me an opportunity to share some of it with someone.

I expect that as I continue to do this, it will give me a chance to help identify (and address more quickly) questions, issues and concerns that the employees are struggling with."

These strategies circle back to the leadership mindset practices we started with in Section One, and brings those into the regular flow of your workday.

10-Minute Leadership Questions:

- *What part of the WHASSUP strategy will have the biggest impact for you?*

- *How will it enhance your relationship with the team and your shared work?*

Journal

Strategic Thinking Time is a Must

I had coffee recently with a new person in my network. He is in the publishing business where he publishes a monthly industry-specific magazine and is one of the primary salespeople charged with selling advertising and building relationships in the industry he serves.

He shared that in his business, each day is like a game of volleyball. The game begins when he arrives at work, when the first volley is his email Inbox. Then the phone calls and meetings come in. The next volley is addressing the issues or situations that are presented by his team. Almost every day goes something like this.

He bemoaned that he is in a constant state of reaction and has very little time to think proactively (i.e., strategically) about his business. He's not able to step away from the noise and constant volleying to consider what's really important and the direction he needs to go next.

As I sat and listened, I saw myself in his narrative and also remembered similar stories from conversations with other business owners. It seems as though we all slide into our role as business owner or leader and the days sweep us away, leaving us wondering, "What did I get done today?"

Here are three steps to think and act more strategically each day, leaving no question about what you got done:

1. **Escape**

   Most leaders have very little quiet time when we can detach from the noise and duck the constant barrage of volleyballs. We have quiet time at home, though most of us understandably don't want to think about business there. Here are some strategies for finding your workday quiet zone: Pick a spot where you are out of reach and away from the noise; take up residence in a coffee shop with no Wi-Fi network; sit in your car with no smartphone and the radio off; sit in a public park.

2. **Schedule strategic thinking time**

   I asked my new friend how much time he would feel comfortable carving out for some solid proactive, strategic thinking. He thought one hour would be a great start. "So which hour of the day will you schedule that on your calendar?" I challenged. He squirmed a little and then said he could make it work from 3:00-4:00 p.m. Don't leave your own thinking time to chance. Aggressively carve out the time on your calendar. This is something you and your business deserve and need.

3. **Buddy up**

   Who do you talk to about your business or leadership challenges and your important issues and goals? If you're like my new friend, you just shook your head, because there is no one. This isn't unusual for business owners or leaders in organizations. One of the top issues leaders face is loneliness. Find a friend, fellow business owner, or coach who will listen, ask questions, and share a perspective. Having this accountability and support is invaluable to thinking strategically and getting out of the volleyball game.

🕐 10-Minute Leadership Questions:

- *Where are some places you could escape to during your work day?*

- *When will you schedule the thinking time in your calendar?*

- *Who will you buddy up with to end the isolation of leadership?*

Journal

Can You Be a Leader 10 Minutes at a Time?

Being the leader of a team or organization entails thinking about the bigger picture of the endeavor and its people, in terms of:

- **Vision** – What does the business want to be when it grows up?

- **Purpose** – Why does the business exist or what role does it play in the world?

- **Culture** – What are the core values of the business and how are they lived out each day?

- **People** – Putting the right people in the right roles at the right time.

- **Process/systems** – What systems or processes need to be in place so the business can deliver better results?

Focusing on these five things is a full time job in itself, but sometimes the dedicated time to do this only comes a couple times a month when talking with your coach, your board, or other trusted advisors.

The rest of the time, especially in the early years of a business, you are not only CEO, but also CBW (chief bottle washer), CHC (chief head cook) and every other C-level position in the company.

The demands are many as you often find yourself in the weeds of ensuring customers are happy, work is getting done, and the bills are being paid.

A client recently reflected on the current state of his business and his place in it. His board had made a firm request for him to start being CEO of the company and to get out of the weeds. As you can imagine, this is easier said than done. The spirit of the request is spot on and exactly where he needs to be to move his business forward towards its goals and beyond. The reality of the situation is a different story, and often times the weeds are *exactly* where a leader needs to be so that there *is* a tomorrow for the business.

Given this reality, how can you step out of the weeds and into being a true leader of your business, team or organization? By taking it 10 minutes at a time.

Here are three questions to ask during those 10 minutes to ensure you're being the leader while also fighting the fires of the day and getting things done.

1. **What am I building?**

   The answer to this question will force you to choose whether you're building a company or just a group that does work and then moves onto the next thing and then the next and then the next.

2. **How do I bring my leader-self to the next meeting or activity?**

    We often settle for second best from ourselves, our team, and the results we get. This question gets us thinking about how to approach the next situation in a way that will build what we are really intending to build.

3. **How do I approach the next task so that I never have to do it or be involved again?**

    Take a few of those 10 minutes to document the process or bring someone alongside of you so they can do it the next time.

As you take these steps, the 10-minute chunks of time should start to grow, affording you more time to dive into those things that only you, as CEO, can do.

🕐 10-Minute Leadership Questions:

- *What are you building?*

- *Where or with whom are you settling for second best?*

- *How will you approach the next task on your list so you never have to do it again?*

Journal

Conclusion: The Final Word

Thank you for taking the time to read this book. I hope it has inspired you to consistently invest in yourself to become a better leader. Whether you invest 10 minutes at a time or make a larger commitment to your journey, you will be rewarded with better outcomes and happier followers.

If you've enjoyed this material and you'd like to expand your capacity to lead and consistently get better and better results, then I invite you to enroll in *The "10 Minute Leadership" Strategy Session*. This is a one-on-one intensive with me that is designed to:

- Lay out your vision for your leadership and the top priority goal you want to achieve through your leadership

- Create a personalized 100-day plan with at least three concrete next steps

- Develop a plan of action to address the key issues or problems you see in your way

The most important thing you'll gain from this experience is the energy and momentum to become the leader you need and want to be.

Imagine what bottom-line results your team or organization will achieve when…

- ✓ Your expectations are clear

- ✓ Employees are truly engaged in the business and have input into the decisions that affect their performance

- ✓ You give employees what they need (as opposed to what they want)

- ✓ You demonstrate character in all your interactions

- ✓ You are disciplined and keep commitments

Are YOU ready to invest a few hours into taking the next step in your growth as a leader?

FOR MORE INFORMATION VISIT:

BrillianceWithinCoaching.com/10minuteleadership

My wish for you is to not only deliver on the commitments you've made as a leader, but also have a more meaningful and fulfilling leadership and life experience.

Wishing you all the best
on your journey,

Jeff Harmon

About Jeff Harmon

Jeff Harmon, ACC, is the founder, president and head coach of Brilliance Within Coaching & Consulting. Brilliance Within was founded with a passion to support those in leadership positions to take their success to new levels and thereby increase the success of those they serve.

Jeff is a leadership coach, speaker and author with 17 years of leadership experience in both large organizations and small businesses. Jeff has either led or facilitated the delivery of over 100,000 hours of business strategy and his vision is to equip every leader with the capacity to tackle each business challenge and live a more meaningful and fulfilled life.

In Jeff's coaching, he brings the best practices of servant leadership and project management to the business owner and executive, helping them to deliver on their most important business priorities, and also to develop as a leader. He brings leadership and operational excellence to the level where things get done.

Jeff studied leadership at the University of Central Florida and the Greenleaf Center for Servant Leadership. He is an Associate Certified Coach (ACC) through the International Coach Federation and a certified Project Management Professional through the Project Management Institute.

Jeff is married to Sandy and has two beautiful daughters, Madeline and Gloria. They live in northern

Made in the USA
San Bernardino, CA
16 September 2014